My Buqala

A Collection of Poems

Pankaj Kumar Chatterjee

Ukiyoto Publishing

All global publishing rights are held by

Ukiyoto Publishing

Published in 2023

Content Copyright © Pankaj Kumar Chatterjee

ISBN 9789360168872

Cover photo courtesy: *https://jazairhope.org/en/do-you-know-the-algerian-female-poetry-of-the-bouqala/*

All rights reserved.
No part of this publication may be reproduced, transmitted, or stored in a retrieval system, in any form by any means, electronic, mechanical, photocopying, recording or otherwise, without the prior permission of the publisher.

The moral rights of the author have been asserted.

This book is sold subject to the condition that it shall not by way of trade or otherwise, be lent, resold, hired out or otherwise circulated, without the publisher's prior consent, in any form of binding or cover other than that in which it is published.

www.ukiyoto.com

To
Ratna Chatterjee

Preface

When I came across the name of 'Buqala' I spontaneously thought to use it in naming my first book of English poetry. And so the idea of "My Buqala" is conceived.

Būqāla refers both to a ceramic pitcher as well as to poems ritually embedded in the traditional, favourite, divinatory pastime associated with women city dwellers of specific Algerian towns such as Blida, Cherchell, Tlemcen, Constantine, and Algiers. In course of time there has been a shift from oral form to a written archive of French and Algerian collections of *būqāla* poems. There was focus on Algerian Arabic oral literature as an expression of feminine cultural protest and resistance to the domination of language policies under French colonialism. In various ways an intimate ritual—one linked to oral form, the divinatory, women's poesies, and the Algerian Arabic dialect—began to carry political meanings during the War of Independence and in post-1962 independent Algeria? Contributing to the circulation and creation of new meanings, forms, and venues for *būqāla* poetry are Algerian radio and television broadcasts, Internet postings, and the publication of the 1962 French poem "Boqala" by Djamila Amrane.

Buqala is a game still practised by Algerian women after daylong breakfast during the month of

Ramadan. They sat in a circular formation with a buqala in the centre. Every woman puts a silver ornament inside the buqala and recites short poems in the form of riddles. After all are finished the recitation a call is made to solve the riddle and one who can solve a riddle is entitled to get the contents of the buqala.

My poems are mainly short in form and so I would like to call them "My Buqala" which definitely may not have anything related to the original Buqala poems. The centrality of my poems is humanity- human nature, culture, sorrow, joy, religion, ethics and in this way more or less everything that can be ascribed to humanity. This is my first venture toward English poetry and naturally I am apprehensive about the reaction that my poems might get from the readers at large.

Apart from majority of the poems of general nature, I have included at the end ten poems on the Ukraine war written by my more than a year back.

Dated , Khardah, Kolkata
The 28th October, 2023
Pankaj Kumar Chatterjee

Contents

Red Letter-Day Of Love	1
Unassuming Nature	2
He Who Knows To Defeat The Shadow	3
Truce	4
Perpetuity	5
Dragonish Death	6
Whose Hand Is Behind The Paw	7
The Story Of The World Below	8
The Realm Of The Sin	9
I Want To Be Torn Into Two	10
An Easy Lesson	11
I Will Be Naked Again	12
Hey The Sun! Go On	13
I Like Daydreaming	14
Time Of Departure	15
Light Bath	16
The Childhood	17
Sin Cycle	18
Darkness Knocks At The Door And Goes Away	19
Evening Sun	20
The Face Of The Religion	21
Fulfilment	22
Vortex	23

A Failed Life	24
Feeling	25
The Light	26
The God Is Busy	27
The Word Of God Floats In The Sky	28
The Thirst	29
Eternal Truce	30
Just Walk On	31
Fossil	32
Is This Love?	33
Nothing Forever	34
Lend Your Ear	35
Last Nomination Paper	36
The Sums With Known Answer	37
Endless River Of The World Of Life	38
Inequality	39
Long Live Slavery!	40
Manifesto	41
The Ascension	42
The Relationship	43
Song Of The Road	44
Ether	45
Triplet	46
Memento Of The End	47
The Cry Of The Age	48
Five Petals	49

Did You Call?	51
Run	52
You Are Not Human!	53
Modern Drama	54
Pebbles On The Shore	55
Poems On The Ukraine War	58
From The Land Of The Comedian	59
From Kharkiv	61
Letter From Ukraine	62
Captive Life	63
The Meaning Of War	64
Ukrainians Knew	65
At Chernihiv - My Mother	66
From The Battlefield	67
On The Phone With Alexei	68
They Didn't Know That Trees Have Roots	69
About the Author	70

Red Letter-Day Of Love

There was no red-letter day in our life.
On a red date
on the leaf of the calendar
if I lift finger and say
we are your Lords-
the calendar leaves keep undulating
with no answer.

The black-letter dates of our heart
revolt and the love pounds its head
on the white stones.

Unassuming Nature

To know how much fire flows
in the proud blood
let's go underneath the tree.
In the dewdrops at dawn
held on the leaves
the fire extinguishes.

Know not
why the nature loves me
and tolerates my cruelty.

He Who Knows To Defeat The Shadow

I saw shadow of the sun.
Also of the moon and the earth.

Never saw the shadows of the stars.

In the logjam of the space
those who know to become light
are worshippers of beauty
and are eternal
like the pole star.

Truce

A tiger is on this side of the culvert.
On the other a deer.
Flowers flow
in the water underneath.
The tiger and the deer-
Will they come to truce?
A million dollar question… ..!

Perpetuity

When the sun sets to the west
I hear the song of death.
Bells on the legs of the fireflies ring:
night after night
death after death
beneath the starry canopy
a mechanical perpetuity

Dragonish Death

The low tide comes after the high tide
and that's opportunity to repay debt.
The opportunist does not understand
the value of the moment
Life gets sold on auction.
The death bids the price.

Whose Hand Is Behind The Paw

Low pressure forms in the mind's sky.
The eyes are reddened.
By the flow of tears.
get erased the marks of nightly kisses.
A tiger chases only after a tiger.
On the bosoms the wounds glow.

The Story Of The World Below

The rain drops fall and the leaves swing.
Water falls from the swinging leaves
on the lower leaves,
on the lower branch,
and finally on the ground

A long black paw comes forward.

The lowly-borne ones don't get the fragrance.

A flag flies on the top of the temple.
Below lies next to the arch-gate
a corpse of unfulfilled aspirations.

The Realm Of The Sin

Ah! The smell of flowers now!

Blood oozes out of the nose and the mouth.

Smelling flowers is now a sin

Those are spoiled

on the way from the garden to the market

in the smell of the sweat of millions of local train passengers

in which the seeds of the blood are hidden.

The flower garden is now covered with blood

I Want To Be Torn Into Two

I am the river.
I don't know poetry.

Even being a poetry
ever I carry
sadness, pain, garbage
and push them to the estuary of completion.

I agree
to be cut into two.

Moses is waiting!

At the end of eruption of all the syllables
maybe I won't rejoin anymore,
because today we carry the history of partition.

An Easy Lesson

When clouds come in front of the sun
I understand that light travels straight.

Even if there are hundreds of obstacles ahead
the adventurer climbs to the top of the mountain
in a difficult winding road.

In the crooked path of life
no light enters.
So people easily
have learned
the crooked way.

I Will Be Naked Again

The earth is naked.
People were also naked
and were happily at one with nature.
Civilization brought the disease of cover:
the disease that cannot be cured by education and culture.
Separated from the happy nature
they get rotten and withered to become alone today
in sickness.

So they open the veil of women
seek the face of naked happiness
in maddened glee.
Illness does not go away.
Unhappiness increases.

Hey The Sun! Go On

Everyone gets his dues in full.
The sun too.

The sun lends light to the moon
and collects interest to the last penny.

One side of the moon is bright with capital of light.
Even after repaying interest
the reverse side remains dark.

Belonging to the same family of cosmos
the moon could not realise its fault.

Likewise the raped woman does not know
trapped in a darkened life
even after repaying the debt of being born as a woman.

The sun sees everything
even keeping the accounts wrong.
A shameless usurer!

I Like Daydreaming

Under the scorching midday sun,
in the bosom of the barren desert,
by the side of a dried up river,
next to the bloodstained raiment of the rapist-
in the daytime with open eyes....

I dream!

Although I know that a dreamless night's sleep means death.

Time Of Departure

Don't stop him who wants to go.
Give as long as you have time.
Don't get entangled in the void left by despair.

Burn the lingering memories.
When the ashes are trampled on,
the footprints will remain
on the threshold of the door
like an immortal question.
Neither you nor he
won't know the answer

Light Bath

In the blaze of fiery light
many things don't become pure.

Yet the light pours itself out
to the point of becoming extinct
over the forest-mountain-river-countryside.

In the last lap of a marathon race
the black man stepped forward.
Loses the white man.
Perseverance
prevails over pride.

The black man in the flood of light
looks white.
Light becomes worthwhile.

The Childhood

The childhood flies
like torn pages of a notebook.

Flying in the air in the sky
sometimes they hit the eyes or the face.

Then I dream
of a new world
of a new civilization
of a new childhood

Sin Cycle

Words thrown into the void do not return.
Wait.
If you don't hear the echo
believe you did not commit sin
because
sin returns again and again.

Darkness Knocks At The Door And Goes Away

Late at night
Once, twice or thrice-
he will stop knocking at the door.

Keep quiet
in the circle within your own circle
with the wisdom, profession, talent, perseverance.

Learn that
one who came
was darkness, not light.

Evening Sun

Before sunset
the sky is covered with clouds.
Before dusk
a darkness reins.

The events are like:
before giving the scriptures
in the hands of a martyr on the gallow
the death knell is heard.

Under the hood
the martyr laughs
like the evening sun
behind the clouds.

The Face Of The Religion

One washes away sins at the feet of idols!
Is this the face of religion?
Like this many questions do not get answers.
The temple bell rings
in the hands of a blind mendicant.
Flocks of devotees cannot have
the reach of the *prasada* (1).
Kangal Harinath (2) sings
'Hari din to gelo sandhya halo....'(3)

[(1) *prasada*- offerings to the deity while worshipping, (2) pseudonym of an ancient Bengali scribe and writer, Harinath Majumder, (3) a line of a popular song written by him, meaning "Oh Lord Vishnu! The day has passed and the evening has come....'.]

Fulfilment

While moving the decimal point to the right
I feel the difficulty to reach the whole from the fraction.
The hope of prosperity is far away...

Under the torn sky
with a torn heart
let's sing protest songs
for ages to come....,

with a thirst for attaining perfection.

Vortex

Even when the ink runs out, the pen continues.

Like running out of breath towards the light.

God has no time to wait.

Time is chasing me.

This is how the world revolves around itself

from darkness to light and vice versa.

A Failed Life

Cartridges ran out.
I'm still walking along the path with the hand on the trigger.

No effort, no perseverance, no experience.

Like rolling the wheels on horizontal paths.

At the end of the day, there is no penny left.

Within the anthill of indolence,
a failed life.

Feeling

The sculptor brings beauty on the face of the idol.
I don't know whether his hand or brush to praise.

The leaves lie next to the flowers under the tree.
Do the leaves know the glory of the flowers?

The branches of the tree lose their beauty.

I could not get through the mystery.

Like the hand and the brush
don't know each other.

Grace does not last forever,
remains only the feeling.

The Light

I know only darkness.
A long way to go to know the light.
I don't know
whether any boat is docked at the port
nor is there any sailor.

But I know-
like fallen leaves of the tree
I have to flow on the river towards the sea
at the whims of the river.

There is no such thing as God.
There is only light.

The God Is Busy

Arranging the flower
one after one carefully
I make the garland.

Feelings of different colours-
I arrange at the bends of the road ahead.

On the way of life
I realise the value of tidying up,

and also that the God has many things to do.

The Word Of God Floats In The Sky

A cloud-veiled moon sometimes emerges
like lightning in the corner of your lips.

I gradually move towards the God.

God's instructions come:

Stop there

and know from the moon in the open sky tomorrow
the hints of the future.

The Thirst

So much light around.
But why is there such thirst?
Why the land of darkness after twilight?

In Kurukshetra to quench the thirst of the *Gangeya* (1)
arrows of Arjuna flows.

The *chataka* (2) looks at the sky
with endless hope.

There is darkness half of the day,
while the thirst consumes the entire day

[(1) Bhishmadeva in the Hindu purana is also called with this name as he is the son of the Ganges, (2) a bird which chirps towards the cloud in the hope of rain]

Eternal Truce

The soul walks through the ether.

Light passes through the void.

A truce is made in the furnace of the time,

between the Life and the Death.

Just Walk On

Is the death dark?

Is the birth light?

Is the dusk the centre of gravity of life?
Maybe or maybe not.

In the maze of light and darkness
it's like walking along a long secluded path,
while understanding life.

Fossil

If you go ahead
a furnace of the burning ground looms large.

If you fall behind
A mirror comes forward.

He-
whose face is deformed
whose back is like terracotta
survives
in incomprehensible immobility.

Is he then
the fossil of the Future?

Is This Love?

In a container without a lid
one puts alms.
Unveiled eyes
see the path of love.
If one expresses greatness by giving alms of love
everyone pours admiration on him.

A thirsty lover
tires himself out
by seeking dreams
in the notches of a naked body.

Nothing Forever

I draw a picture.
Then I erase it.
All out of fancy.

Sadness of the colour-
why will the brush care?
It is my slave
with whose blood I make the colour.

One day
I will not stay-
neither the paint nor the brush.
Around the stage of life
will roam only the smell
of the bare earth.

Lend Your Ear

I saw the source and estuary of the river.
Yet while writing its biography
I encounter wrong words at every step.

But the flow of river is faultless.
Gold is grown in the fields by its side.
Life is abuzz in the cities and ports.

The raft of hope comes near down the river.
All the failures go to the estuary.

To find words today among all these
I fail to find my failures again and again.

Today I understand the riverine civilization
forgot to stand by the river.
The river flows with a chestful of sorrow.

On the surface of the scattered leaves
lend an ear, you will get an answer.

Last Nomination Paper

I am helpless.
The throat is pressed from two sides.
I did not understand his purpose till now.
To the tune of his flute made by my own hands
I danced like a snake,
I ate milk and banana.
Then was confined in the charmer's busket....

Today is the last day of
filing my nomination paper.
But there is no caution money.

The Sums With Known Answer

There is no wind.
Still the decorated kite is flying.
Loh! Suddenly its string is cut.
It floats towards the horizon.
Picking sticks in hands
runs the kite-runners.
In the thicket of thistles on the banks of the pond
is found torn bloodstained raiment of an woman.

The sums of known answer
end this way.

Endless River Of The World Of Life

Mother said:
Eat before you go.
I look,
once towards the kite,
then towards the empty plate

Mother doesn't come.

There is still a mother in the world of hunger.

I think in dreams:
If I get thirty rupees
I would have helped
Jesus to be caught.

Inequality

Along the equator
someone is plying a saw.
It will divide the world into two.

Above is the kingdom of haves,
below is the kingdom of have-nots.

How long can they stay together
and remain each other's eyesore?

The question remains
Who will get
the Earth's true orbit.

Someone from behind
raises hand
to veto.

Long Live Slavery!

Where are the bucks
so that I can laugh and play like you?

The light of charity from the moon
goes to the exact address
touching the top of the jungle.

Tearless eyes
burn in the sunlight.

I plan to turn the Five of Hurts
into the Jack.

A life like others' is not for me.

Manifesto

Dry leaves fallen from the tree
sing today a song of protest
with the harps in the hands.

The tree within the tree
There is a lot of wealth.

Skeletal roots bulge out
As if the tree is hanging.

Dry leaves
sing today a song of protest

The Ascension

Lunch at noon.
It's quite a fun.

But we haven't learned to call it siesta!

So under the scorching sun
we have to work hard.
Beckons Modern Times!

The Relationship

If I don't get anything
at the disposal of my hands
I use mind as the pathfinder.

The mind goes first.
I'm behind.
Definition of relationship
gets its shape.

Song Of The Road

At the bends of the road
I become alert.

If the spine is erect
there's nothing to fear.

When the curves
are straightened,
I lift my head.

All worries about distance
fade away.

Ether

I get confidence
while staying with the sky.

In spite of all provocations
I don't extend hand
towards the sky.

The sky knows to come down.
Then I talk with it alone.

Triplet

(1)

I won't return.

While biding goodbye,

I brought the recyle-bin too.

I am not an absconder

in the diary of forbidden, cursed Earth.

(2)

Going to the sea,

I ask – what should I draw?

There is hustle and bustle among all the colours.

Birth and death melt when the ocean churns.

The water-colour of the life becomes clearer.

(3)

Today the cats have become tiger

and the tigers…..!

None notices that

the nails and the teeth of the cats did not change.

Similar happened to the tigers.

Memento Of The End

Thought that
with the help of powerful men
you could scrape through?
Then why are you scared
in the lonely dark alleys?

The powerful men
under the booze of wine
forget the world.

Have you forgot the poet's words-
If none comes even hearing your earnest call
walk alone?

Oh! The forgetful mind!
Fly towards the blue hues of the distant horizon.

The sailor of the last trip
will not fail to call you.

The Cry Of The Age

The leader elephant of the herd calls in shame.
Silvery moon in the sky.
It falls to pieces.

We then burn
in the fire of shameless civilization.

Five Petals

(1)
I dreamt of three cats.
In reality I saw the same.
Still I am afraid
of comparing dream with reality.
If the cats turn into tigers!

(2)
The price of mutton is high.
That of chicken is less.
Ours' is lesser.

(3)
I forget the known roads
and am afraid of unknown ones.
The garden is full of flowers.
Yet the time is unfavourable.

(4)
Buy two, get one free.

If number of paths increase in this way
I'll stop treading paths.

(5)
Not interested to insure my house against fire.
The agent still pursues.
He doesn't understand that
I'm fine in the house of inferno.

Did You Call?

When the storm arose
the balcony was covered
with the flying leaves of the trees.
Did you call me then?

There was still light.
Happiness was in the air.
There was no expression in the eyes.
There was no melody in the song.

Outside the feeling of
possession or dispossession
there's only the call of the universe
inside the heart.
Have you ever called me?

Run

After the morning,

straight into the crowd thronging the evening candle prayer.

Midway is the pale face of the noon.

In the darkness of the night the fire-flies embrace the stars.

Light and shade of memory in the colourful afternoon.

The manuscript of the nightmare gets lost

in the crowd of tourists on the Nile.

A slender stooping body runs after the wildfire.

You Are Not Human!

O Almighty!
You always lose to humanity!

Towards the frozen body of the raped
you don't cast eyes.
We cover the naked body
with her torn veil.
Before that we carefully wipe
all the infected red wounds.
Let not burn the satan's blood
in the pure fire.

O Almighty!
You lose again and again to humanity
as you are not human.

Modern Drama

A group of boys in the morning
went with open sword in the hands.
Everyone was quiet.
In the afternoon they went the opposite way
with open sword in the hands.
Everyone was quiet
waiting for the heroes and the heroines...
They know very well
modern heroes and heroines.
They don't come in front of the stage.
Still ruled by the rules
spectators wait.

In the last game
everyone will exit by clapping together.

Pebbles On The Shore

(1)

I'll break the door, not the window.

I'll break the obstacle, bring the light in.

        Let the river flow.

(2)

The bees went mad with the fragrance of flower.

The vehicle of the fire-brigade is at the garden's gate.

        Doesn't find water

(3)

The last leaf has fallen.

Yet the traveller recognises the tree.

He fixes the burning incense sticks.

The arrival song rings at the bottom of the tree.

(4)

The water now rolls from the bottom to the high.

Why blame the water? If the mountain gets upside down!

(5)

At the end you have to come to the house of sin,

burning in the fire the sight of assuming eyes.

(6)

I keep the scale in the balance.

If I manage to get some profit,

I forget my self-identity.

(7)

The fragrance doesn't attract, rather the good look.

The cool shadow doesn't fill the heart.

The stomach gets full with the thirst for the sunshine.

(8)

Even if the skin is dry,

the corner of the mind does not fold.

The iron of consciousness is still hot.

(9)

Such a dwarf I've become,

that the eyes don't get up to the window.

Rather they are stuck to the

rat-killing poisons spread on the floor.

(10)
My sleep breaks in the midnight.
I cannot accept the obstinacy of the darkness.

(11)
Hearing the midnight knocks on the door
I stand with raised hands.
I know that he will break the door.

(12)
The truce with the icy air
has ended.
Now the war is with the sunshine

Poems On The Ukraine War

(written more than a year ago)

From The Land Of The Comedian

Morning, 23 February 2022.

Lines in front of all shops.

Most people came back empty handed.

Lines in front of the ATMs are longer.

Failure here too, money runs out.

Excited people are confined to their homes since morning.

No, it's enough!

This time there is a longer line in front of the military office.

Alas! Weapons are limited. Not everyone has military education.

So again failure.

People did not stop.

Enrolled in the volunteer army.

They don't fear the risk of danger.

Far from the battlefield

It's a picture of Lviv on Ukraine's western border.

This is comedian Zelensky's land!

From Kharkiv

After finishing the book
I was going to pick up another book-
Missile splinters
took one eye.
Back from the hospital,
I stood in line. I want weapons.
Else I will be completely blind.

Letter From Ukraine

"We read the fairy tales they read.
We see the the movies they watch.
We live in the same world.
Do they want its destruction?
Why can't they stop it?
Alas! Many people don't want to.
They don't value freedom
neither theirs nor ours.
They are all mere slaves."

This letter might have been addressed to a child,
who would become a normal person, not a dictator.

Captive Life

In the subway, we are the prisoners
in the hands of the Russian troops.
Sometimes someone is called from above.
I don't know if he would return!
Russian troops release the old and the sick
through the Green Corridor.
Again through some false Green Corridor
people are going, maybe for the last time.
Children are orphaned.

The Meaning Of War

War means not only killing and violence.
War means opportunity-
not to kill,
to bring back wounded people from the face of death,
to serve people,
to stand by the struggling soldiers,
to supply relief items,
to return the lost child on the mother's arms,
to recognize oneself in the mirror of the heart.

So, the war is not just a war.
Ukrainians will win.

Ukrainians Knew

Ukrainians don't know-
when the war will stop
when they can return home?
when they will be reunited with their family?

But, they already knew-
Kiev did not fall in ninety-six hours
as predicted by America,
knew that
the lost ground has been regained,
knew that
the days of panic are coming to an end,
and knew that
there is a price to pay for freedom.

At Chernihiv - My Mother

Which is the source of which sound?
Rocket? Fighter jet?
New mine explosion?

My old mother now knows all.

In a few days, black hairs on the head-
all turned white.
Mother has learned to live with the war.
Now in spite of a series of queer sounds
she can sleep at night
and plant new flower seedlings in the garden.

From The Battlefield

Anastasia's story:

the heart is saddened to hear,

when she says:

a lone Russian soldier

was about to rape her.

She struggled and went on running away.

She saw the knife of the Russian soldier piercing her back.

Anastasia! Please go home!

I don't want to hear further!

I'm still in the warfront!

On The Phone With Alexei

A friend died in the battlefield.
Another in rocket attack on Kharkiv.
They are happy now.
But we are fighting the satan in the hell.

Occupied or free?

Russia claims:
Occupied territories are fascism-free.
Truly free-
from a normal and happy life.
A diabolical captivity!

They Didn't Know That Trees Have Roots

Displaced people
from one country to another,
over the ages fly
like the migratory birds.

Displaced Ukrainians do not know
when will they return to their own land
and see the oak tree
left in the garden.

It might have been burned by missile fire.
Shoots coming out from under the black stem
announce that there is life and there will be.

About the Author

Born in 1953 in North Bengal. Graduated in Physics. Worked in a bank for 28 years as an official. After voluntary retirement, pursued a career in financial consulting for two decades. Started writing during the COVID-19 lockdown. Published books include 'Bastarer Pathik: Verrier Elwin o Anuradha Gandhi, 'Abar Taliban', 'Bismrita Ananya,' among others. Translated from French to Bengali, 'Staliner Divan' (with assistance from the French Institute), and a collection of translated poems from Ukraine titled 'Yuddher Samayer Kobita: Ukraine Theke.' Translated from English to Bengali 'Phulmat of the Hills', the only novel written by Verrier Elwin, and the Bengali translation of the French book 'Vie the Beethoven' by Romain Rolland. Translated from English to Bengali the newly discovered Chekov mystery drama 'Drama on the Hunt' as 'Shikare Rahasya.' In addition to this, a collection of 18 short Bengali stories translated into English is being published.

www.ingramcontent.com/pod-product-compliance
Lightning Source LLC
LaVergne TN
LVHW041628070526
838199LV00052B/3284